WOOD MOUNTAIN POEMS

ANDREW SUKNASKI

Photo By   Jessop
                                            Nokomis

Macmillan of Canada/Toronto

ISBN 0-7705-1388-3

Printed in Canada for
The Macmillan Company of Canada
70 Bond Street, Toronto M5B 1X3

—to the memory of leila hordenchuk and john nicholson

CONTENTS

INTRODUCTION

The hill country of south-west Saskatchewan, including the village of Wood Mountain and the Cypress Hills, has a history as exciting and picturesque as any area in Canada. Before nineteenth-century settlement, warlike Blackfoot Indians rode against their enemies here; buffalo hunters from the U.S. ranged across the American border into Canada; whiskey-traders from Montana sold rotgut to Piegan and Blackfoot. In 1876, when Sitting Bull crossed the Indian "Medicine Line" to escape American troops, the Royal North West Mounted Police established posts at Wood Mountain and Fort Walsh.

The Cypress Hills, tucked away on the Saskatchewan-Alberta border, are a geologic and ecological treasure trove, because at their highest altitude (4,500 feet) they escaped the last Ice Age, some 40,000 years ago. Wood Mountain itself is raised above the surrounding prairie, on a 3,000-foot plateau. The area is both farming and cattle country, and also the setting for Andy Suknaski's *Wood Mountain Poems.*

This book is in no sense a history of the area, although it does deal with Wood Mountain people and history. Nor is it an autobiography of Andy Suknaski, although his own life is both marginally and centrally involved. More than anything else, the poems are a clear look at people and places of Wood Mountain, seeing both past and present simultaneously with a kind of double vision. The poem-viewpoint shifts abruptly, for time exists as a territory to explore; the dead are raised, in the sense of re-creating them on the now pinpoint of here: after which they return to the past, having lighted up a little place in the mind of whoever knows about them.

There is nothing flashy or sensational about these poems, no verbal surprises or gymnastics (apart from the elasticity of time), and certainly no overt struggling on the page to make poems out of what might seem most unpromising material. But there is a sense of place here that I find unequalled anywhere else. It is a multi-dimensional place, with an over-riding feeling of sadness because so much is lost.

But perhaps strangely, the effect created by these poems is not entirely nostalgia and sadness. The affection for all things that are, and have been, running through them rises above humdrum daily incident and becomes finally an understated triumph. For instance, the incident of the farmer who goes mad because of drought, and harvests a great quantity of thistles ("40 bushels to the acre/the best crop I've had in years")—that incident is symbolic of this queer triumph, in which nothing turns out the way you think it will, but is nevertheless a human achievement.

Despite the impressive long poem "Homestead" opening the book, its total is far more than the parts. And having lived inside these poems while editing the book, I feel a full citizen of Wood Mountain.

AL PURDY

when the buffalo are all slaughtered, the wild horses all tamed, the secret corners of the forest heavy with the scent of many men and the view of the ripe hills blotted by talking wires, where is the thicket? gone. where is the eagle? gone. and what is it to say goodbye to the swift and the hunt? it is the end of living and the beginning of survival.

CHIEF SEATHL

WOOD MOUNTAIN POEMS

Mandel's
observation of
"identity or patchwork,
a now patched up
of then and no
longer the same
that gives Juknust's
work its
   authenticity"
   p 50

HOMESTEAD, 1914 (SEC. 32, TP4, RGE2, W3RD, SASK.)

i returning

for the third spring in a row now
i return to visit father in his yorkton shack
the first time i returned to see him
he was a bit spooked
seeing me after eleven years—
a bindertwine held up his pants then
that year he was still a fairly tough little beggar
and we shouted to the storm fighting
to see who would carry my flightbag across the cn tracks
me crying: *for chrissake father*
lemme carry the damn thing the
train's already too close!

now in his 83rd year father fails
is merely 110 pounds now and cries while
telling me of a growing pain after the fall
from a cn freightcar
in the yard where he works unofficially as a cleanup man
tells of how the boss that day
slipped a crisp 20 into his pocket and said:
you vill be okay meester shoonatzki
dont tell anyvon about dis
commeh bek in coopleh veek time. . . .
father says his left testicle has shriveled
to the size of a shelled walnut
says there's simply no fucking way
he'll see another doctor—says:
the last one tried to shine a penlight up my ass
now son
no one's ever looked up my asshole
and never will
never

while we walk through the spring blizzard to the depot
i note how he is bent even more now
and i think: *they will have to break his back*
to lay him flat when he dies   *wow .*

in the depot
father guards my bag while i buy two white owl cigars
and return to give him one
we then embrace saying goodbye
and i watch him walk away from me
finally disappearing in the snowflake eddy near a pine
on the street corner
and then remember how he stood beneath a single lightbulb
hanging from a frayed cord in his shack
remember how he said
my life now moves to an end with the speed of
electricity

ii mother

her ship sails for the new land
and she on it
the fare paid by her brother in limerick saskatchewan

dancing in the arms of some young farmer
she remembers her polish village
the day her mother is fatally struck
by a car—
she remembers being 14
when world war one begins
remembers how she and another girl walk 12 miles
to work every three days
shovelling coal onto flatcars for sixteen hours
before returning home
along the boundaries of wolves (their eyes glowing
like stars on the edge
of the dark forest)
she remembers the currency changing as the war ends
her money and several years' work
suddenly worthless one spring day

all these things drift away from the ship carrying
her to the unknown
new land

iii father

arrives in moose jaw fall of 1914
to find the landtitles office
is given the co-ordinates for the homestead east
of wood mountain village—
and he buys packsack and provisions for the long walk south
sleeps in haystacks for the first few nights
(finally arriving in limerick
buys homesteader's essentials: axe saw hammer
lumber nails shovel gun bullets food
and other miscellaneous items)
he hires someone with a wagon and horses
to drive him to the homestead
builds a floor and raises one wall that day
and feeling the late autumn cold
nails together a narrow box in which to sleep
the first night

the following morning
he rises through two feet of snow to find
all his tools stolen (except for the gun bullets
and knife he slept with)
he searches for a spot on the hillside
to carve out with a blunted knife
a cellar
in which to endure the first few years—
he nails together a roof with a stone

philip well is his closest neighbour
and they hunt together
and through long evenings
play cards by light of the coaloil lamp
spin tales of old country wanderings
to survive 40 below winters till pre-emption time
is up

when the landtitle is secured
and a more suitable shack is built—
father walks six times between moose jaw and
the homestead
till haggling civil bastards give him the title
each time
he carries a $10. bill sewn inside his pocket across
the heart

iv *parting*

the day i walked fearless between horses' trembling feet
my father watching with hands frozen
to a pitchfork
is clearer in my memory
than the day he and mother parted
—she leading the children through the fall
stubble to wood mountain

in the following years
all i knew of father was the lonely spooked man
whom i met each autumn
in the back alley behind koester's store
while winter descended from the mountains—
it seems he always came during the first storm
and tied his team to the telephone pole
(their manes and nostrils frosted)
he always pulled a side of pork from the hay
in the wagon
and placed it on my sleigh

parting
we never found the words
simply glanced at one another's eyes and turned
something corroding the love in my heart
until i left wood mountain one sunday afternoon—
running away to the mountains
for what i thought would be forever
until another spring
i returned to see father
eleven years later

v the funeral

sofie in winnipeg
sends each member of the family a telegram announcing
the death of sister eve

mother who is 66 at the time
rides a greyhound bus from moose jaw to brandon
all night
father and brother louis drive from yorkton
arrive in brandon the night before the funeral
and get a hotel room—
louis goes out and buys father a pair of pants
and a shirt
returns wondering: *how the hell will i get*
father out of that sweater he's sewn himself into?
back in the room
he goes to the bathroom and turns on the water
and returns to subtly introduce the idea to father
who will have no part of it
louis loses his temper and pulls out a pair of scissors
from a shaving kit
and wrestles father to the floor (cuts him out of
the old sweater
while father cries:
okay okay—i'll take a bath)

the following day
the family is all on edge
everyone wonders how mother and father will respond
to one another
after 18 years of silence—
louis drives father to the funeral chapel
where mother is already viewing their daughter
they park outside
and father nervously climbs out as the chapel door opens
(he freezes

while mother emerges and also suddenly freezes
both stand motionless for 30 seconds and then
begin to run toward each other
they embrace
and she lifts him off the ground
he is 79 at the time)

vi birth certificate

carrying it in my pocket now as father carried
the worn $10. bill across his heart for the landtitle
i have crossed bridges of cities
hoping to find salvation
have gazed into the dark rivers of
spring where others found love
hoping to glimpse the face of some god—
and stopped by grey-eyed policemen

produced identification and tolerated their jokes:
what do these letters and numbers mean kid?
where is this place?
is this all you have?

vii epilogue

my father once said:
i might have murdered you all and gone
straight to heaven

and having arrived at all these things now
what is to be done with you and love
father?
what is to be done now with that other man who
is also you?
that other man so long ago on a hot summer day
far too hot for man or beast
the day mother at the well with the rope
frozen in her hands watches louis
who has ceased haggling with you
sadly carrying a bucket of staples to the barn—
you father something frightening

slowly sweating and walking after him
you slowly raising a fence post above your thoughts
swimming in familiar rage
over that day's fence posts' improper spacing—
louis stopping suddenly for some reason
not looking back
but merely gazing across to tall wheat growing
beyond the coulee's black shadow
(you suddenly stopping too and seeming afraid
and then lowering the fence post
as you turn around and return to the picket pile
to continue sharpening poplar pickets
with your newly sharpened axe)
that other man beating mother with a rolling pin
by the cream separator one morning
she pregnant and later sleeping in the late afternoon
to waken from a dream while the axe rises
above her grey head
her opening eyes staring into the eye of death
you father slowly turning away once again frightened
and ashamed

you once warning us of that other man within you:
when these things happen to me
do all you can and help one another save yourselves
from me

that other man once sharpening mower blades
when brother mike plays and suddenly tips
a bucket of water used to soak blades—
that other man suddenly drowning in black rage
grabbing a long scarf from a coat hook in the porch
then seizing mike to knot the scarf around his neck
and around the end of the grindstone's pulley
bolted high in the porch corner
the trembling right hand slowly labouring to turn
the crude sandstone
(mother and sister sofie fortunately arriving just in time
to fight you and free your son)

father
i must accept you and that other dark man within you
must accept you along with your sad admission
that you never loved anyone in your life
(you must be loved
father
loved the way a broken mother loves her son
though he must hang in the morning
for murder)

viii suicide note

silence
and a prayer to you shugmanitou*
for something
to believe in

Eliot's skepticism

*shugmanitou: coyote in dakota indian language

WOOD MOUNTAIN ALMANAC

the amber moon
seems a huge plate
rolling down the west ridge
of three mile butte—
the point of turning back
for rcaf training jets from moose jaw
(the southern boundary
and a buried missile base moments away)

drinking tonight in the west central pub
men joke about the old times
and their quaint ways remaining
as a living almanac

a myth grows:
the full moon—
the ideal time to seed
slaughter
and procreate—
calves are best weaned
at the beginning of the full moon

in the careful act of procreation
point your wife's head north
for a son—
south
for a daughter

one of the rangers from the south says:
hell
my wife and i have tried all directions
and we've still got 25 sons

JIMMY HOY'S PLACE

gee clyz
all time slem ting hoy would say
when he got mad at some obnoxious drunk
stirring hell in the cafe

all time takkie to much
makkie trouble sunna bitch
wadda hell madder wid you?

gee clyz hoy would mutter and scold the man
would shake his small grey head and disappear into
the smoky kitchen to scramble some eggs for the drunk

gee clyz
all time slem ting something would whisper
in the back of hoy's mind
as he sat and smoked his pipe through the long afternoons
in the empty cafe
maybe immersed in a dream where the years became centuries till
a child's coin rapped on the scratched counter
drew hoy from his dream

hoy's early history is uncertain
though some speak of a time when he first arrived at
the old post and built a small cafe and livery stable
and how drunk halfbreeds often rode into the hamlet
to lift hoy onto a table and make him dance
as they shot up the floor

when the railroad came through
and the hamlet was moved five miles north
hoy built a big new cafe complete with false front
the text reading:
HOTEL
wood mountain cafe & confectionery

back in the thirties
hoy threw hank snow out for creating a disturbance
snow had hopped off a freight
thinking a song might rustle up some food in hoy's place—
seems hoy was a bit thin himself and the song nothing new
so he escorted snow to the door
saying: *gee clyz*
all time slem ting

hoy's place was where men drank coffee and told stories
like the one about the time charlie bloiun handled
the village's only holdup
how a killdeer cowboy saw one western too many
and thought he might rob bloiun's store—
following an afternoon of beer in the west central
the man got his shotgun and tied a hanky around his face
and entered the store
while old bloiun counted his money
and whispered: *stickum up*
bloiun briefly pausing to look over his glasses
long enough to say: *pete—you better put that gun down*
before you hurt yourself
and then continued his counting while pete crept out
somewhat embarrassed

hoy's place was where in boyhood one came to know death
when men ceased joking
as someone arrived with first news of men like the jealous agent
from another town—
how he imagined a lover for his beautiful faithful wife
until one day he left a note on the grain scales
saying: *i think it'll be better this way for all of us*
and then walked his .22 behind the elevator
to perform what some believe is the most creative act

hoy's icecream and chinese calendar girls were something to dream
    about
on hot july days of summerfallowing
were something to remember as one woke falling
against the twisted wheel of lovenzanna's tractor

george tonita bought at the auction sale
following the funeral

hoy's place was where we waited on friday mailnights
to glimpse the train's first black smoke beyond the snowfence—
as kids we were fascinated by the engineers and the brakemen
while hoy brought out their steaks and mashed potatoes—
the way they flattened mashed potatoes into thin layers
squared off like dominoes fascinated us
while we searched their eyes for the glow of distant cities
till hoy came saying: *leddem eat—go outside and play*
gee clyz
all time slem ting

JIM LOVENZANNA

i remember sitting in jimmy hoy's place one sunday
listening to old lovenzanna and others recalling stories
about the thirties
lovenzanna spoke of the time before he moved to the village
how he and a neighbour planted crops four years straight
though nothing grew (the land slowly drifting away)
how the neighbour grew sad and spoke less each time they met
and finally lost faith in faith
no longer speaking at all in the end—
lovenzanna remembered something as though it were a dream:
i was driving past his place one day
it was cloudless and bright and very hot that day
and i saw the threshing machine going full blast
and nick sweating beside it with a huge rack load of thistles
i felt kind of funny and thought maybe i was seeing things
anyway i stopped my team and walked over to him and said
"nick—what the hell's up?"
nick's eyes looked like twin moons as he grinned and answered
"threshing jim—must be going 40 bushels to an acre
the best crop i've had in years"
lovenzanna said the mounties arrived the next day
and took nick away to weyburn—
he returned a few months later and the following year
the mounties found him driving his binder
through a dust storm (once again harvesting thistles)
when they approached him
he pulled a monkey wrench from the tool box
and began waving it at them—in the other hand he waved
a crumpled sheet of paper and shouted their way:
look godammit
i'm not crazy and i have proof i've bin to weyburn
now what the hell do you bastards have to prove you're not nuts?

another spring years later
lovenzanna said to friends drinking coffee in hoy's place:
before i die i want to harvest the biggest crop
that's ever been seen in the south country

that summer
summerfallowing on a new quarter added to his prairie empire
lovenzanna moved to another field
it was a hot july day as he made the first round
slowly falling asleep at the wheel he drove
into an abandoned root cellar in the farmyard on the field's edge
(late that night men from the village found him pinned
under the tractor
with a crumbled doorframe across his chest)

in the autumn a dozen men got together to combine the wheat
for the widow
they built a floor in the old barn for the last 5,000
of 33,000 bushels harvested

the evening mrs lovenzanna served the last supper
one farmer said:
too bad old jim ain't here to see it all in the granaries
mrs lovenzanna nodded and
a bottle of whiskey no one had noticed before
was being held next to her heart
she smiled and placed the bottle on the table—and said:
a little of something jim would have given the kids
this christmas

as a farmer finished pouring a glass for each man
they raised their glasses and said:
well—here's to old jim

SOREN CASWELL

as gods of a vanished tribe
caswell's rusting model-a's were another world
where one hid while playing runsheeprun
old caswell fiercely moving through gasbarrels
was something to fear while gleeful smashing of carwindows
ceased and one ran to hide in lovenzanna's coulee

caswell's speech in the village hall and the yearly movie shown
by the greysuited man from the implement company
were something to look forward to when we were children
the trees and grass of ontario farms were greener
than anything we knew

in the village two thirds deserted now
caswell spends his days pottering alone in the garage
some days sells a few gallons of gasoline
and each afternoon saunters over to the pub for a beer
before returning home to his silent supper
no longer permitted to drive
he walks now
and following the meal
returns to the garage to dawdle away an hour or two
where he sometimes scrawls out a letter ending with the faint
illegible signature—
then retires again to the pub for a couple beer lasting
till closing time (he no longer wears his hearing aid
and seldom speaks—is merely a smile in the corner)
late in the darkening night he ambles home
and the street lamp next to the romanian church is a star
guiding him as he no longer notices the boarded up
houses along his street

IN MEMORY OF ALFRED A. LECAINE

wood mountain and indian summer
still here
where my childhood ghosts move in the tall grass
taking over the half-abandoned village—
the last few days before going west
i repaint two of fred's faded paintings:
a pair of brown horses rearing against high green hills
in the reserve
in the distance beneath the horses
cattle peacefully graze in a coulee

having finished the work
i sign *fred lecaine* over his faded signature in a corner
and apply a clear varnish to protect everything
before lee soparlo helps me nail the paintings back up
on the false front of charlie bloiun's old store

next day (sunday) a cloudless day
lee his two sons and i drive to the reserve
to see the lecaine cemetery
in a clearing among poplars and willows on a high hill

we park and walk to the cemetery where a tall white cross
shines
lee points to the hills and says:
there were cars all over the hills and in the coulees
must have been over 200 people at least
they came from montana and north and south dakota
there were people from alberta
there were twelve pallbearers
six guys from the reserve
five fellas and myself
from the village
after we let the casket down into the box

we placed fred's hat on top
before nailing down the lid

a gopher whistles while we comment on the view
opening out from the cemetery clearing
with the sioux indian cemetery visible on the next hill—
we return to the truck
hear the weather report on the radio:
snow storm in the north is now moving down across
central alberta and saskatchewan
and will arrive by nightfall in southern regions

below in the valley chief billy goodtrack
and his sons are stacking the last hay bales—
while we pass they all wave
billy smiling the way he smiled one night in limerick
when he scored our only goal
in the last hockey game we played
alfred lecaine played defence that night
and joked: *if those indians don't take it a bit easier*
i'll pull out my telescopic tomahawk
then we'll show em—eh lee

the following spring
some of us left home to find something of the world
fred and others talked about

LEILA HORDENCHUK

1

yesterday three of us
drinking beer in assiniboia's franklin pub
talked about leila hordenchuk
and her fall from a runaway horse
how she lies motionless and unconscious now for three days
with little hope

many rounds of beer and long silences
and young butch thomas her cousin saying things like:
why do these things happen . . . why her?
she's only seventeen

and john soparlo the wood mountain elevator agent
steering our thoughts to other things knowing
the unanswerable moves us close to tears
recalls old reverend dumitru erina's gravestone
set next to his wife's—
dumitru's text reading *died—196*
the last digit impossible to engrave now
now that dumitru lives into the 70's

last night john left dumitru with weekly groceries
from assiniboia
and told him of leila's fall

today dumitru silently seated in the motionless rocking chair
gazes east beyond the window far
over the dying village—thoughts drifting far beyond
the broken corner post and crude flat stone
on the hordenchuk farm by twelve mile lake
while something stirs through his distant thoughts—
something of the homestead whispering in the language of wind
along eaves to become

listless murmurings within the late afternoon dream
in the pool of memory mirroring leila's face
the day he baptized her 17 years ago
and still beyond her
the sad old face of dumitru's grandfather who thrived
on corn meal cottage cheese goat's milk and hard work
and lived to be 130 years old
back in bucovina romania

2

they say the day before it happened
you spoke of the dress you would get for the graduation

months later
you still lie motionless in that dark sea
and do you sometimes hear bells . . . leila
bells that rang in the church far across the lake?
do you sometimes see the face of your grampa vasile tonita
who's been there many times
in that darkness—
old vasile of whom they often said:
vasile's down with asthma again
is in the hospital in assiniboia
they say the family's bin called in . . .
and of course vasile as always
returned to harvest another crop

leila . . . do you sometimes see autumn sun
across the lake
or wild geese flying south?
do you sometimes hear grampa tonita softly speaking again
as he did months ago:
leila . . . this is your grampa tonita speaking
if you can hear me leila
squeeze my hand—which you did
opening your eyes
the day the nurses said
there was no hope at all

3

leila . . . wherever you are beyond
that corner post
where all our names are written
i hope your uncle walter thomas
sometimes plays his harmonica for you—
blowing out a thousand butterflies
while he crushes the stars
under his right foot
keeping time

PHILIP WELL

prairie spring
and i stand here before a tire crimper
two huge vices held by a single bolt
(men of the prairies were grateful to a skilled man
who could use it and fix wooden wheels
when the craft flourished)

i stand here
and think of philip well found in his musty woodshed
this morning
by dunc mcpherson on the edge of wood mountain—
philip well lying silent by his rusty .22

and i ask my village: *who was this man?*
this man who left us

in 1914
well and my father walked south from moose jaw
to find their homesteads
they slept in haystacks along the way
and once nearly burned to death
waking in the belly of hell they were saved by mewling mice
and their song of agony—
a homesteader had struck a match and thought he
would teach them a lesson

well and father lived in a hillside and built fires
to heat stones each day in winter
they hunted and skinned animals to make fur blankets
threw redhot stones into their cellars
overlaid the stones with willows
and slept between hides

father once showed me a picture
nine black horses pulling a gang plough

philip well proudly riding behind (breaking
the homestead to make a home)

well quiet and softspoken
loved horses and trees and planted poplars around his shack
when the land began to drift away
in tough times well bought a tire crimper
and fixed wheels tanned hides and mended harnesses
for people

and later (having grown older and often not feeling well)
moved to wood mountain village
to be near people who could drive him to a doctor
if necessary

today in wood mountain
men's faces are altered by well's passing
while they drink coffee in jimmy hoy's cafe
no one remembers if well had a sweetheart
though someone remembers a school dance near
the montana border one christmas—
well drunk and sleeping on a bench in the corner
while the people danced
well lonelier than judas after the kiss
(the heart's sorrow like a wheel's iron ring
tightening around the brain till
the centre cannot hold and
the body breaks)

LOSHKA

loshka*
the silver grandmother teaspoon
you gave me for christmas
and all dreams beyond
could once have lured me away in a time
like this
when words falter and lag
seeming deadwood in the blood
rivers feeding the ocean in the heart
but not now
no
not the possible perfect poem
of unrequited love
poets dream about beyond things
such as loshka
we fill with earl grey and
snap shut
brewing you a strong cup of tea
and me a weak one
for my hopeless belly—
no not loshka
glowing in the image of all beyond
or the kingdom
of sad women's eyes ogling the knight
sent on an ancient journey
by some wounded king
no
not for me
the fabled journey turning our love
into a jester's jingle
i will not be
fooled again my love

i only ask for faith
greater care
and gentle words when possible
to cradle
this fragile thing between us
into the future

*loshka: ukrainian for spoon

CHAAPUNKA*

drinking beer again in trails end
with gus lecaine and james lethbridge
gus tells of chaapunka
chaapunka all legs and long sting
on delicate wings
of a summer evening in southern saskatchewan

chaapunka and followers near twelve mile lake
and a man on foot
returning south from moose jaw and stopping to
enjoy a long piss—
chaapunka and inevitable companions zeroing in
the man quickly whipping his pecker in
and bolting for the tall grass and cattails to hide

chaapunka circling in bewilderment and humming in
his high pitch: *zzzzzzzzzzzzzzzzzzzzzzzzzzzzzzzzz!*
whichashsah li dookteh yah?
meaning:
where did this fulla go?

james lethbridge laughing and ordering more whiskey
while i ask:
who was this fulla gus? a homesteader?

gus laughing: *no—fulla musta bin sioux*
chaapunka spoke dakota and the fulla understood him

*chaapunka: mosquito in dakota

MASHTEESHKA*

mashteeshka curled tightly into a white ball
in his burrow
his long ears tuned in to the frequency
of shugmanitou's soft footsteps above

cold wind gathering over the old post curves
right into the burrow entrance
mashteeshka shivering and curling even tighter
mutters in broken dakota: *whali dootecktoo okashnee hew?*
where the hell's this draft coming from?

mashteeshka—the true jester
his humour surpassed only by shugmanitou

*mashteeshka: rabbit in dakota

THICKFOOT

comical old thickfoot
capable of drawing a laugh from the most serious
clergyman's dry dialogue

a northwest missionary once asking
"thickfoot . . . have you not felt
like a great sinner at times?
do you not feel deep sorrow
for some great sin you committed long ago?
do you feel in your heart
that you need to be forgiven?"

oh yes missionary . . . me big sinner
me much sad

ah . . . i thought you must feel this way
sometimes

oh true . . . missionary

thickfoot . . . if it is not too much to ask
what is this great sin you mourn over?

thickfoot grave and confessing
"one time me and my people
we fight sioux
me have plenty bullet
fight six men who no have more powder
me weak in heart like woman . . . say

no good medicine kill men
who no have powder
and bullet
me kill only two
let rest run away
me could kill all . . . this big . . . sin
missionary
ole thickfoot should be forgive
for big
sin"

MISHMISH

anonymous indian tribe of the northwest

1

mishmish
me ole indian sit by campfire
dream . . . like woman fish float in stream
fish who wait for food come in mouth
mishmish too old snare rabbit
young men bring me food
no many buffalo
mishmish grandchildren hungry . . .
sun be nest in birch
who float like canoe on mist
young men get ready hunt
me hear they be say
mishmish too ole
better put mishmish on horse
when we come back . . .
time mishmish ride to nudder hunting ground
huh! mishmish big hunter when young buck
one time in moon of frozen leaves
kill moose 17 hands high
one arrow!
huh . . . mishmish to die like ole squaw
choke with piece green hide
must be kill
when mishmish try kill savage beast
hummmm . . . what kill
what me kill
what kill me?

2

mishmish grandchildren
they be run from coulee . . .
grandfather! grandfather mishmish!
there be big bear
with big nest with snow on neck
he eat saskatoomenahnah menisuk

3

hah . . . mishmish this be sign
big medicine
mishmish fight
put feather in white hair
for each man mishmish kill
take ole tomahawk
go down coulee

eiyaaaa hiyehhh ehh ehh
eiyaa
hiyaaaaaaaaaaaaa huhh huhhhh

eiyaaaaaaa hiyehhh
eiyaa yaaaaaaaahuh
hiyeh hiyeh yehhhh

4

mustahyah . . . mustahyah
here in the moon of ripe berries—
do you hear grandfather mishmish
singing his sad song in honour of death?

mustahyah . . . teeth stained bright red
while you clawless and old feast well
here in the moon of ripe berries—
do you see the tomahawk rising?

mustahyah . . . who do you think
will sleep in the moon of frozen leaves—
you . . . or mishmish?
do you not feel the cold blue breath

of windago under every
step . . . as mishmish walks toward you?

5

ROAAAAAAAAR!
cry . . . HIYAAAAAA!

fierce eye fixed on fiery eye
TOMAHAWK!
crushing through bone . . .

ROAAAAAAAAR! SWING!
of great ball of fur cuffing tomahawk free
and clean through air

MISHMISH
further enraged
fists clinched SOCK!
CUFF!
SLAM!

GRANDFATHER MISHMISH
thinking a lightning thought
me capture ole bear
show hunters
me still BIG HUNTER!

jumps back and runs to camp . . .
MUSTAHYAH SNORTS "GOODBYE"
returns to peaceful berries

6

mishmish and hunter's sons
crawling soundlessly through grass—
only the sound of wind

only the song of the cricket
while mustahyah
crushes crisp leaves and berries

in his mouth until MISHMISH
gives the SIGNAL . . . twelve lassos land
tightening around mustahyah's neck

boys struggling in halfwalk halfdance
leading MUSTAHYAH
back to the camp

mishmish slowly walking behind . . . remembering
mishmish one moon of ripe berries
dance SUNDANCE like this

7

sun be
go down behind camp
ole man bear he be quiet now
maybe sleep . . .
we peg him down good
kill him soon
feed us all

mishmish tired now
sit by campfire
alone . . .
smoke pipe and enjoy smell of willow twigs
who burn

KECHE MANETO
mishmish thank you for bear
thank you for all
you give mishmish good life
give mishmish good horse
who know good trail to KECHE MANETO
mishmish tired
be ready for what come
when hunters come back through birch

eiyaaa eiyehhh
eiyehhh
eiyaaa eiyehhh
hehhhh hehhhhh
hehhhh . . .

THE FIRST COMMUNION

the weathered chapel on the reserve and white cracked paint
trying to remember how big it seemed
those first two weeks of summer holidays (preparing for
the first communion)
and remembering a whitehaired man driving us to the reserve
in the black meteor each morning

—we played softball with the indian and halfbreed kids
between lessons
while on the hill beyond left field
shugmanitou stood silver against the daily blue sky
and watched over us—how it rained the night before
the first communion
and that night the young indian boy playing left field for us
was struck by lightning while going home after confession
and the following morning we ran through green poplars down
the old wood mountain-fort walsh trail to stop dead
before priests covering him with a red blanket—
after our first communion
clouds covered our blue sky we thought would endure forever
and the black meteor carried some of us back home
to wood mountain

GUS LECAINE SPEAKING OF GRANDFATHER OKUTE

i grandfather okute

trails end pub in wood mountain
and near closing time
a weak bulb shines above us while
soren caswell sleeps dreaming in his lonely corner

gus lecaine's eyes seem black pools
all light being two diamonds frozen there
while he slowly recalls a story from his boyhood on the reserve
when his father was still alive and chief:
my father tole me bout a sioux scout ridin in a coulee in montana
he said wen the scout spotted custer's men on a ridge
all dere metallic tings guns buttons and everything woz
shinin like gold in the sun

in a gentle voice gus speaks lovingly of grandfather okute
90 when he and other old men with horses and women
and travois bearing children
cross a stream near the camp (distant warriors crying:
come brothers
it is a good day to die!)

when the families reach the silver stream beneath high sun
gus remembers the moment from his grandfather's story:
water catching light like an ocean spray
water like a million diamonds shattering across the old
and young faces

grandfather okute remembers the scout returning and saying:
it is all over now
we can return home

okute remembers the fires still being warm
and the water still boiling in the pots and food being ready—
gus says: *that was how long it lasted*

the sioux lost merely four men
all werc annihilated on the other side—
gus tells of how one father laviolette questioned the truth
of old chief john lecaine's story:
this is not possible—it defies the law of average

chief lecaine countering:
well then how about david slaying goliath
how do you account for that story with your law of average?

lights dim and we are grateful to roger the new barkeeper
for patiently listening to the story
and letting us drink an extra half hour
we leave unfinished beer for the ghosts at trails end
turning his head to finish his beer
gus nods and smiles remembering something—the two diamonds
in his eyes vanish forever

NEZ PERCÉS AT WOOD MOUNTAIN
for dennis lee and john newlove

> *we came from the earth*
> *and our bodies must go back to the earth*
> *our mother*

toohoolhoolzote (nez percés prophet)

1

that place where the soul goes
to lie among buried bones
and ancestral dreams
when we leave our boyhood towns farms and hills
to journey to the plains—
and they too
the nez percés who survived
to flee up to wood mountain
believed something of this movement
rendering one
faceless

2

heinmot tooyalaket
or better known as young chief joseph
whose father rose to chieftainship in dawn
of nez percés along clearwater river

old chief joseph opening his heart to white men
lewis and clark 1805
nez percés feeding the explorers' horses
that summer
while the two men canoe to the pacific

old chief joseph and his people migrating later
to wallowa valley
the new home
green vast meadows
with forests abundant with game—
winding waters and a bluegreen lake

in 1871 the father dies
and chieftainship passes to young son joseph
who shares his father's hospitality
toward white men—
white men later lust for gold in nearby mountains
and finally rustle nez percés' cattle and ponies
(white bird's unheeded warnings
becoming a bitter reality)

gold seekers and politicians twist truth
turning nez percés' honour and name into a jingle—
the truth being
that the gold seekers are the rustlers
and of course
the great father of america gives nez percés
the usual ultimatum:
move to lapwai reserve or suffer the ensuing fate—
the bloodthirsty bluecoats

3

moccasin telegraph telling of wood mountain
the possible refuge
the peaceful santee dreams and sleep
and the teton sioux (their refuge)

young chief joseph dreams of these through
the uncertain sleep of mountain nights

nez percés
finally moving up through the northwest to
the bearpaw mountains
miraculously battling the bluecoats for a thousand miles—
their chief surrendering one night
while white bird and last followers creep through
a dark coulee beyond bluecoat sentries
(nez percés fleeing north to wood mountain
as chief joseph gives last speech
steeped in abandoned hope
to later die of a broken heart)

4

i am tired of fighting
our chiefs are killed
looking glass is dead
toohoolhoolzote is dead
the old men are all dead
it is the young men who say yes or no
he who led the young men is dead
it is cold and i have no blankets
no food
no one knows where they are
perhaps freezing to death
i want time to look for my children
and see how many of them i can find
maybe i shall find them
among the dead

5

wood mountain
the winter is cold and the game has vanished—
santee and teton children cry: *tacko eena* . . .

somewhere north of the montana border
the last nez percés are met by sitting bull
walsh and 1000 teton warriors ready for battle
(all are startled by the appearance
of the bedraggled nez percés)

nez percés
death ambling clothed in rags—
children with arms and legs snapped by bullets
wounded children tied and hanging from
the saddle horns
while men and women and horses are nothing
but a walking graveyard

sitting bull and his men befriend the broken people
take them home to lodges
near the old wood mountain post—
nurse them back to health again
and later provide lodges and a place to call home
somewhere to restore something of a dream
a face and pride—
white bird finally affirming some night
before the teton chief and others around a campfire:
i have no country
i have no home and i feel
i have no people

MELVIN GREENE/ONEIDA INDIAN FIGHTING
FOR A PLACE TO DIE

the earth was created with the assistance of the sun, and it should be left as it was . . . the land was made without lines of demarcation, and it is no man's business to divide it . . . the earth and myself are of one mind.

chief joseph of the nez percés

pale bowlegged ghost of james wounded horse
floating high over wood mountain
i now summon you
to the poem's witness stand

toronto . . . friday october 25th 1974
today in the courtroom
of the immigration appeal board
they bitterly dispute melvin greene's
rightful place to die
melvin
son of an oneida mother from ontario's
thames reservation
and an american onondaga born in new york state
melvin still believing
in his 68th year
his home is his mother's as is
the iroquois custom
always

the immigration special inquiry officer claims greene
is an american
by virtue of birthplace
new york state
that he does not have a canadian residence
and was once convicted
of a crime involving *moral turpitude*
for which he served 15 years in prison—
thus he must be deported

melvin speaks in oneida
translated by an interpreter to the board:
i consider the oneida to be my tribe
i have never considered any place else
as my home . . .

there is no record of his citizenship
anywhere
his documents are the oneida elders' *word*
on where a person belongs—
although there is
an old undated document recording the lineage
of the cornelius family
the new english names remotely familiar
to melvin
who knew his relatives
by their indian names

pale ghost of james wounded horse
what do we do with melvin greene . . . ?
melvin
travelled like james
james leaving wood mountain's sioux indian reservation
to go to the pow wow and stampede
in wolf point montana
once a year
for forty years . . . then returning with friends
and relatives
arriving in time for another pow pow
at the wood mountain stampede
james and all
exercising their aboriginal right
to cross the border freely with their personal belongings
without a single incident

pale ghost . . . how do we tell this appeal board
that it is not a matter of
being canadian by indian law
or an american by white man's law?
how do we tell them
that it is a matter of *being* . . .
that it is a matter of a law beyond
all these things
that if justice is to prevail
there can be only one decision:
MELVIN GREENE MUST BE FREE TO DIE
WHEREVER HE WISHES

justice + law not the same.

THE TETON SIOUX AND 1879 PRAIRIE FIRE

I consider it impolitic to give Bull a reservation in our country. He is the shrewdest and most intelligent Indian living, has the ambition of Napoleon, and is brave to a fault. He is respected as well as feared by every Indian on the plains. In war he has no equal, in council he is superior to all. Every word said by him carries weight, and is quoted and passed from camp to camp.

a letter to the minister of the interior by major walsh

sitting bull
a legend flowering along the lips
of aboriginal people telling the story
around campfires across the unfenced plains

sitting bull
among the ghosts of my youth
i try to imagine him
the lines around his eyes reminiscent
of shadowed prairie trails in the late afternoon sun
where he sits musing by a lonely campfire
some evening outside the rice valley lodge
in wood mountain—
what did he feel or think
smelling the southern plains burning above the missouri
wood mountain incised by the moving sword of fire
may have looked like a sundancer
beneath heatwaves
the dancing plains fastened by smoke coiling to
the dark orange moon
while he and his people fled to seek refuge
in the wood mountain post

in the police post
major walsh agrees to feed the teton
till bull's two messengers return with news
of the others who journeyed to reservations
near fort buford in the states—
the deceived messengers return with tobacco gifts
and a goodwill missive for the chief
they weave tales of the happy wellfed people
—which the other teton are
for several days anyway
rejoicing over extra rations distributed
before the northern messengers arrive

whatever offered will be taken away

THE SUN DANCE AT WOOD MOUNTAIN (1879)

the sun dance
and blue smoky hills of 1879

the plains cree called it *the thirst dance*
but the teton might have renamed it
the hunger dance
as they began to eat their starving ponies—
they must be praised for rebuilding
the rice valley lodges with scorched poplars

they cleared away long burnt grass for
a place to dance
formed a circle under the high sun
the young dancers within
each warrior bearing four vertical incisions
across his chest
where two leather thongs were affixed
beneath skin and muscle
the young warrior thus attached to the tall centre pole

they drew faith from the power of the human wheel
turning from sunup to sundown
chestmuscles stretched while teeth rasped
the willow whistle blown
to forget the agony of the dance

when the first warrior broke free and fell
unconscious
and died at moonrise
three horses were killed that their ghosts might
carry the soul to greener hunting grounds
in the heart of wakantanka

and wakantanka rightfully honoured
by the dance
was still powerless in the tide of
white man's greed
(and unable to save the sacred tatanka*)

*tatanka: buffalo in dakota

POEM TO SITTING BULL AND HIS SON CROWFOOT

spill water's child
her horses ran four times
red leaf

indian summer
and poplars flare into the unimaginable
oranges reds and yellows

in the nearby willows
a pheasant's rusty cry rasps the silence
while i walk on this high hill—
sioux cemetery markers lean like signposts pointing
to distant constellations
names read like haiku:

brown eyes
held at bay
yellow leaf

wood mountain descends along heat waves to fade
where pinto horse butte begins
in the west

wounded horse
james wounded horse who taught me how to play pool
in my boyhood when we used to set pins
in vasile tonita's pool hall on friday mailnights—
once wounded horse leapt like a struck rabbit
high above a tenpin ball hurled his way
by some jester who wouldn't wait for the pins to be up
(i still remember how fear crossed his eyes
and moved me
the way his metal marker now mirroring the sun
casts my thoughts to sitting bull and a dream
where the lives of these people begin
where something in my life seems rooted here)

sitting bull
who dreamed of the possible
union of indians spanning the plains west to
the shining mountains—
i wonder if his dream floated like frosted helium
before his eyes
the day sun gleamed bright across waiting guns
while men dragged him feet-first from the tepee

while he rose to
crumple to the ground with his son
did his life really flow before the darkening light
his years in these southern hills
older than the meaning of name
and the gods i will never know
or the lying faces of men who betrayed him
giving him an ultimatum:
starve or surrender to the enemy

his was not the peace
his brothers the santees found here
a peace they said he too would finally find—
he did not share their sound sleep
beneath sweet smoke of willow bark flaked
and drawn through the pipe

he may not have had time to remember
the words he left us with at wood mountain:
the great spirit provided for both white and red men
but white man has grown powerful
and defies the gods—
is trying to undo all wakantanka has done

wounded horse
the engraved text reads on the cheap
government issued marker—
i listen to the wind moving through barbed wire
wired to steel 8 horse eveners driven in the earth
(eveners that once strained
beneath harnesses and horses while homesteaders broke
the land)

leaving the graveyard
i recall seizing bear's words:
if you truly believe you live or die in a day
then so do i

then something inside me whispers:
who ever listened to the dreamer
or a poet

THE BITTER WORD

from fort walsh
colonel irvine brings the bitter word
to sitting bull at wood mountain
makes clear the government welcomes the teton—
yet they must not expect provisions
or food from canada

sitting bull proudly replies:
when did i ever ask you for provisions?
before i beg
i will cut willows for my young men to use
while killing mice to survive

in the spring of 1881
sitting bull gathers his remaining 1200 sioux
and treks to fort qu'appelle to make
the final request for a reservation—
inspector sam steele tells them
the great white mother wishes them to return
to their own country
(a rather curious view of a people
whose meaning of country changes with
the migrations of tatanka)
steele politely refuses the request
and supplies enough provisions for the return
to wood mountain

death by summer is certain
while irvine makes sure
provisions and seed never arrive

seeing the migrating game
sitting bull knew the tatanka
would never return
though his people dreamed of white tatanka rising
from the subterranean meadows others fled to
(hideous shrieks of red river carts grating in
their ears)

he must have sensed the hunger to follow
which was exactly what the authorities hoped for
on both sides of the border

SANDIA MAN

shugmanitou
a humble prayer to you for strength and light
to illuminate dark faces of the lost
gods among these southern hills

north wind along eaves murmuring something
to the old telegraph office
louis vezina dragged north from the old post
to live in
while building most of wood mountain village
from 1929 into the early thirties—
something along eaves nudging thought toward
meaning along margins of time
and a question: *where to begin?*

sandia man
leader before the meaning of the word
your back hunched against cold wind from the pole
the family and others following you
to finally arrive among tall conifers on glacier's edge
(cave in a hill by the bluegreen lake
mirroring your face each morning
—until you move on some autumn day
to arrive somewhere else still
to sleep and dream
about mammoth and the warm body
of your woman spooning your bent back)

sandia man
and your dream of grandfather in asia
grandfather whose ghost you followed ascending
blades of broken light
up through conifers of northern asia to all beyond
to finally arrive here on these plains
where your grandmother slowly ambles through the dream
the simple stone tools falling one by one
from the worn sack of skin till
the last spear point clinks against bone
the dream ending and you wakening to cry: *ughhh!*
in the morning
you check your spear to find the point gone—
before even eating
you flake out a new one slightly fluted near the base
for a firmer tie
something slightly new though
it will be another 10,000 years before complete change
the clovis point and a new people across the plains
followed by folsom man still another thousand years later
ice retreating north
water replaced by marshland abundant with fish
another staple to vary the simple diet

sandia man
silent ancestor of a people who travelled over
northern trails beaten by mammoths and later buffalo
and then finally by one anthony henday
sharing brazile tobacco with the blackfoot
to write in his daily journal august 18 / 1754
of a blackfoot man in central saskatchewan:
i dressed a lame man's leg
he gave me a moose nose
which is a very delicate dish
for my trouble at this place
a mineral spring as cold as ice

sandia man (pale ancestral ghost across face
of shugmanitou laughing me out of an evening dream)
november 1973 and wood mountain village moves into storm
two thirds of the people gone now
and snow drifts into dunes over the tall grass reclaiming
the place—
something knuckles its cold way along eaves
and seems to whisper: *you are returning*
what kind of faith lures you here to build a home
within the dying?

wind again along dry walls and wail of shugmanitou
near dumitru erina's farm on the village edge—
shugmanitou's mate redoubles his cry to the full moon
high over twelve mile creek cutting through soparlo coulee
where at creek bend
lichen grow bright on five stone circles
(burrow within a circle by the creek's edge
where she will spoon shugmanitou's body in sleep)

NEEHHRESON

neehhreson*
white belly and white tail the young follow in the night
tail pointing high to the full november moon
as he sails gracefully over barbed wire—
the whole sky becoming a small silver point
pressing neehhreson to the faded stubble

hunter slashing the throat
while neehhreson emits the cry of a new born calf
forty head of wild cattle converging on the hunter and his kill
(the hunter only saved by leaping onto a huge stone
once burnished by wood mountain's tatanka)

naked hunter who waves red coveralls a whole afternoon
till hunters travelling the distant road
finally notice him

*neehhreson: antelope in dakota

SOONGEEDAWN

soongeedawn*
the full moon burning tunnels through your soft brain
while you arrive in wood mountain to prey
in silent coulees

soongeedawn
will you ever forgive us for poisoning offspring
of shugmanitou

spring and your bleached spine hangs on a barbed wire
while wind sings through headlights of a charred ford
in the nuisance ground—black ants build an empire
in your ribcage
and three bluebells grow on a hummock
where something struggles
as though trying to send a fist
up through the earth

*soongeedawn: fox in dakota

WEST CENTRAL PUB

we smoke white owl cigars
and drink white wine—
john moneo says:
lil jimmy rogers—
now he made some fine lil records
the lil bugger could sure sing—
was a fine poet
(they'll never touch him
in a thousand years)

a young buck we know
walks in with a girl
none of us have ever seen—
moneo quotes service:
there are strange things done
in the midnight sun . . .

                         of wood mountain
adds lee soparlo

then a man from killdeer enters
wearing a pair of pants
that seem nothing but seams and patches—
i remark to john and lee:
in first year university
if you take philosophy
the dizzy fuckers talk about an ole ship—
the boards are replaced board by board
till a question plagues the mind—
is the ole ship there anymore—

at what point does the new ship
replace the old one?
then i talk about those pants
with patches seeming three layers deep—
wonder if we ever become something else
completely changed

the man with patched pants has overheard me
and asks:
where the fuck did you get your education?

i guess it begins now
i reply

INDIAN SITE ON THE EDGE OF TONITA PASTURE

1

the meadow lark's song
heralding spring
waters lazily flowing from wood mountain's peat moss springs
to become twelve mile creek running north
through this coulee where i caught fish
and swam in boyhood unaware
of three rings of stones that nearly vanished
beneath dust from a field
lee soparlo's father worked trying to feed his family
in the thirties
and this great centre ring and something
holding me around my heart the way
a wired stone anchors
the cornerpost of the nearby fence running north
and west to the village
where i grew up—i claim these things
and this ancestral space to move through and beyond
stapled to the four cardinal directions
this my right
to chronicle the meaning of these vast plains
in a geography of blood
and failure
making them live

2

vasile tonita 70 now
and once again riding the spirited stallion
his sons have never ridden
counts his spring calves

and searches for a missing cow south in the coulee
where a hawk slowly circles under the high sun
while i stand here listening for the possible
ancestral voices
as the wind passes rustling
the rosebushes and taller grasses
by the creek

and i try to imagine those who passed here so long ago
possibly becoming this dust
i breathe
try to imagine how prairie could once become a brown sea
following a sound greater than thunder
a sea shaking the earth
beneath an indian's feet
and how his daily breath became a prayer shaping all thought
toward food for a family—but that time has passed
the marks of those who saw it few
and seldom found
except by the rare eye
spotting a stone
here
and a stone there
following a hunch and using imagination
and the good sense of one's feet
till the circle is completed
as lee soparlo did one spring
placing a wired anchor stone beneath the cornerpost
then straightened his back with pain
his eyes suddenly blurring
and then focusing on the first stone he walked toward
studying the place
till all three circles where the tepees once stood
were discovered

and who were the ancestors
that camped here?
only the wind knows for certain
though maybe they were the gros ventre the ashkee
some of whom died from hunger
along with assiniboine middlemen
journeying down from york factory that summer of 1716
when the english ships carrying provisions
did not arrive early enough . . .
or maybe they were some of the assiniboine
met here by their brothers
who traded on the missouri
contracting smallpox for the second time
at fort union in 1837
doing the same as others before them
fleeing northward
believing they could thus escape the dreaded disease
the whiteman gave them—but the assiniboine failed
their 1200 lodges were reduced to some 400
less than 3000 people surviving
they were only one of many tribes
thus diminished . . .

more of a Pordy poem

or perhaps here
a few santee families gathered
around an evening campfire
to listen to a grandmother's story forty years later
a story telling how a whiteman
named isaac cowie
working at fort qu'appelle
found himself without cowpox vaccine
when the great smallpox epidemic of 1838
began to spread
and how remembering the old way of doing it
he went to old breland a métis
whose grandchild had been vaccinated
and begged him for a lymph from the child's arm
was granted enough healthy vaccine
on windowpane fragments
to protect everyone at the fort
the people becoming the next source
supplying sufficient vaccine to protect all people
about surrounding lakes
and visiting indians at the fort
who became the third source journeying to the southern plain
and remote places like touchwood hills
and wood mountain
these people doing their work so well
that not a single case of smallpox
occurred among them—
the northern plain
was another story . . .
and maybe the santee grandmother knew
the story of the christ child
and was able to give it still
another meaning
making it live

Someone else can do the thing he can't do

PRAIRIE PHOTOGRAPHS

i dust drift scene, manitoba

summer of 1930
another dust storm has passed
someone with an eye for remote beauty
leaves a sagging shack
to arrive somewhere—
frames the dust drift scene
with an old camera:

spray of black leaves across a delicate tree
hunched against a dust drift
powerful arcs
mirroring intense light
where all green things begin
to vanish
and all remaining will too
when the grasshoppers arrive

ii gleichen, alberta

kae turner tall and beautiful
a worker at old sun school
on the blackfoot reserve

one sunday
someone photographs her
she is seated on a fence post
and holds a tall thistle like a lover
against her botticelli thighs—
the prairie is a shell
where she stands

the year is 1931
and russian thistles flourish—
they are more precious than all
spices silks or gold
for they will keep some family's horse
and milk cows alive
another winter

iii dust storm near okotoks, alberta

july
1933
a wall
of earth
a mile high
advancing
from the north—
harry thomson snaps
a photograph
and returns
to the farm house—
refills the coal oil lamp
before his wife lights it
so the family can share
a simple meal
it is 12 noon

iv shanty on grierson dump, alberta

july 1934
and the low sun casts a bright light
across the wall
papered with newspapers
the *evening in paris* sign above the bed

tells something of poetry
and art in the man's soul—
one carefully notes
the embroidered pillow
suggesting the gentle love of a grandmother
back on a failed farm
some grandmother who took pride
in her craft
fighting arthritis twisting her hands
into unimaginable forms

one is haunted by the patch
on the man's eye
and must praise and love him
this proud man
turning one good eye to a new life
weaving baskets to survive
the lonely winters

VASILE TONITA

vasile tonita
who for more years of work than his wife cares to remember
delivered milk daily to homes
in wood mountain—
and if some evening the milk did not arrive
one always knew the reason
vasile invariably cursing himself hoarse
straining to rein his runaway horses
once every two years . . . shattered milkbottles
scattered the last quarter mile home
mostly concentrated at the railway crossing
where i once saw
his twowheel cart leap skyward
vasile's feet and wooden floor
making contact
some twenty feet
and fifty milkbottles later

i was his last milkboy
and for several years each day after school
i rode his favourite horse *tiny*
to bring home the milk cows from the east pasture
coming to know a covey of partridges and places
where they took refuge
in cover

startling them once from a rosebush
they scared my horse
to a dead stop . . . me
gracefully sailing over his small head
my vision clearing in time
to see them wing over the tracks and into
the great horseshoe coulee
where vasile wintered his cattle and horses

later vasile taught me to drive a tractor
and during the summer holidays
i helped him harvest and hay
always making enough money to buy clothes shoes and books
with enough left over
to help my mother buy coal and wood for winter—
one autumn i had enough left over to buy an old .22
and later hunted rabbits
on winter weekends
always proving to be a hopeless shot
and sometimes tried my luck with the partridge covey
only missing again and again

and coming to know the triangle the covey flew
i sometimes followed them
on a sunday afternoon—
followed them from the snowfence to the horseshoe coulee
and on to the old soparlo farm
chasing them still further to the edge
of caraganas in the romanian graveyard where
they seeing me a half mile away
always flew the village edge home
to the tonita pasture

it occurs to me only now
their circular flight contained secrets
of a world i never knew—
only now am i able
to imagine the covey's slow dying and eventual renewal
through the newborn each spring
a bird often becoming coyote's feast

i imagine the covey slowly dying with the village
and yet expanding
till still another covey forms
leaving for still another coulee
the way village families have moved one by one
to further places
and the way vasile's children leaving home
married
till all were gone—
only vasile and his whitehaired wife left
in that big lonely house
across from the abandoned
cpr station

PRINCIPAL IN A PRAIRIE TOWN

he was the whitehaired man
who had been thrown out
of some montana college—
so he came to wood mountain

he only lasted a year with us—
hell
we'd never seen such a deadbeat

the kids never learned a thing
(so the people said)
as they scraped together
a historical pamphlet about the indians
on the reserve

yeah
well that was all so long ago—
though we still reminisce
about the hallowe'en carnival he dreamt up
and how the boys
nailing up the booths
sneaked up behind him and nailed his shoes down
to the hall floor
(and we still remember
how the crazy bugger glued bright crepe paper
between windowpanes covering spotlights
made from big tomato cans
to give us our first lightshow
during the christmas concert—
and it's the last concert we've had
now that we have better principals)

now our children all pass
and go on to university to learn new neat things
they tell us about at christmas

THE SNAKE

1

his green eyes on the homestead of another man
he is not man enough to find his own—
he and his wife form a plan

they move in with an old timer and she cooks
and washes all the clothes
(later attends to sexual needs of both men
the old timer believing: *heaven could never be this good*)

several months later he gratefully transfers his land title
to their name
and the simple heaven continues several more weeks
till he is given the boot—
the story being: *the couple no longer needs a hired man*

thus the homestead is attained

2

they raise wheat pigs potatoes and a son as hopelessly
homely as his old man

to the bewilderment of all the neighbours
the son marries the most beautiful farm girl around—
following the reception and wedding dance
the son's father sleeps with the bride
and later says: *my boy didn't marry her for love*
he married her because he couldn't find a hired man

the old man continues sleeping with her
delighting in her youth and softness
and occasionally treats her to her own husband

she endures this for three weeks
before running away
forever

BILLY BROWN

mee beeg eendian—beeg eendian
beeg tough eendian billy brown would announce
as he entered the west central for another afternoon
of drinking

he always wore a blue shirt that seemed
a shade lighter than the autumn sky beyond yellow poplars
also wore a buckskin vest from his younger years
when he toata and soak brown were the best bronc riders
in the south country

when billy's wife went blind
he built a poplar railing from their shack to the well
and outhouse

only a few years ago after one of billy's benders
a rancher found him following a blizzard
billy on his knees by his porch door
one hand frozen on the doorhandle
and the other gripping a cracked bottle of pilsner
near his heart

i love buckin broncos
but love women more he says as he reminisces
about his rodeo days

talks of drinking with pete knight and soak and toata brown
in moose jaw the summer of 1930
and how they were heading west to the calgary stampede
how he wondered whether to return to wood mountain rodeo
or travel west with them

and he says: *now here was my problem*
am i going to go to calgary buckin broncos
or am i going to return to wood mountain and my good woman?
this was the predicament i was in
now what would you have done?
anyway i said to the fullas in moose jaw
"i'm goin with a woman in wood mountain
and i'm suppose to go back to wood mountain
if i don't go back to wood mountain
maybe she'll disown me"

and so he bought a ring and returned home
married the young woman and lived happily for thirty years
and never has seen the calgary stampede
now lives alone in the village
still makes the odd purse or pocket wallet

he spends most of his aftenoons in the trails end
drinking calgary beer or whiskey and water
has all the memories he needs here
to sustain him—
arrives nightly at the town well where the children once played
in the playground
slowly pumps a pail of water to make another lonely pot of coffee
and slowly ambles coughing all the way home
carrying something more than merely a pail of water

JOHNNY NICHOLSON (1925–1974)

1 north to saskatoon

remembering johnny now that indian summer of 73
riding with him north to saskatoon
for another load of farm implements and combine belts
and stopping in assiniboia for breakfast
with his father and mother in law—
remembering johnny smiling while ole geedo* muttered
into his bowl of porridge:
johnny . . . hiss too kold here in ssiniboia
hiss be diffrent klimet frome vood montin
i tink mehbee me n babah† . . . vee go back to farrm in spring
orr mehbee prroperty in mooz jow

remembering johnny laughing
while babah leapt from the stove and leant over the table
geedo ducking like a pheasant when hunters approach—
remembering johnny laughing deep from the belly
as babah knuckled her wooden spoon dripping hot porridge
babah willow thin and trembling in
gentle slavic rage and uttering:
prroperty . . . ah tehbee sracku tom geedo!

remembering johnny—the twinkle in his eye a distant star
and babah whose rage evaporated in a single moment
while geedo's smiling eyes became a sunset
over his empty bowl

2 the farm

the snow has not arrived yet
and johnny susan and i stand out of the wind by
the huge garage
he and dora built last summer—johnny chuckles
and proudly smiles while his son rory rides
a small motorbike down the hill to the barn—
and susan runs up crying . . . *my turn rory! my turn!*
johnny saying: *i built the bike myself this summer*
built it with my new arc welder
i took a couple wheels off an old side delivery rake
and used scrap metal for the frame
the motor's from an old mower—
rory and susan have a lotta fun with it
and i enjoy watching them

dora calls us in for supper—and putting the bike away
by the wall where all tools neatly hang on nails
we hear a nighthawk's cry from the distant coulee—
it is unimaginable that in several months
johnny will be drinking beer in wood mountain's trails end
and listening to ranchers recalling old deaths
after his older brother dies—someone saying:
most of these prairie deaths come in threes
it is unimaginable that in the new year johnny
will be labelling new fanbelts and telling dora:
this one is for the tractor dora
and this one goes here on the combine . . .
remember this dora . . . in case something happens

3 geedo after the funeral

assiniboia—the end of another summer
and geedo 82 has just finished his evening beet soup
his appetite gone
he ambles out into the backyard that is still green
and stops by the shovel stuck in the ground where
potato plants have withered—
and babah by the kitchen sink
looks out of the window to see geedo simply standing there
gazing south to wood mountain
maybe imagining the place north of their homestead
where their son helped johnny fix fence a week earlier
the place where johnny fighting for one more breath
crumbled to his knees
to die
in his brother in law's arms—geedo looks up at the sky
and then grasps the shovel
slowly sinking it deeper with his right foot
before he has even turned the dry earth
a nighthawk's cry beyond the abandoned clay factory
reaches him . . . he is already falling and babah
clasping an empty soup bowl to her withered breast cries:
geedo . . . geedo . . . geedo

*geedo: grandfather in ukrainian
† babah: grandmother in ukrainian

DEPRESSION HIDE BUYER

no more cattle to be bought
the old jew settles into hoy's place for the winter
and plays cards each evening
after buying hides each day in the lumber yard

listens to stories between deals
like the tale of old reegill:
i shoot cahyoote
i mees—i shoot heem in sem place
i mees agen

once a lean farmer throws three coyote hides
on the table—
the jew paws them reflectively
while the pensive farmer waits for the grading
the old jew finally says:
deez one iz primarry
deez one is ooordinary
and deez one iz jewst a fooking doog!

JERRY POTTS

*(jerry potts was a legendary halfbreed guide
for the NWMP during the force's early days)*

1

jerry potts
crow black eyes
and moustache a raven feather
wrapped around the upper lip—
in the famous photograph
he stands
as though the west wind
is curving around his shoulders
as though the wind
has suddenly shifted
and a northeast wind
twists
his hips and spine

jerry potts
better known as *kehyokosi*
in his time
among the plains indians
where his legend began—
kehyokosi
beloved bear child
born somewhere
before 1840 to *namopisi*
crooked back
of the bloods
and andrew potts from scotland
bear child
who later rises to fame
and is
an honoured warrior
among the blackfoot

his father
working for the american
fur trading company
is a factor
at fort benton the day
a young clerk
haggles with a blackfoot
who finally bears a grudge
out into a willow grove
hides
and waits patiently for sundown
and revenge—
the clerk leaves work early
and old andrew potts is left
with the daily chore
closing shutters
the blackfoot finally sees
an arm reaching into evening twilight
and empties a buffalo gun
into the old man's chest

bear child's story
becomes vague at this point
some claim
he is then adopted by alexander harvey
a wild
and lusty trader
on the upper missouri
a man
who abandons the boy
five years later
the boy
then adopted once again
by andrew dawson
a gentle scot

others tend to believe
the more colourful story:
bear child a young boy
skilful with a rifle
and how the evening his father dies
he follows
the murderer's trail day and night
back to camp
where the blackfoot
arrives whooping and boasting
about his act—
how the boy shoots him dead
with a single shot
in front of the man's own tepee
how the boy is honoured by the old men
for his bravery
and is taken in and taught
the blackfoot way of life
how to hunt
and track—
how he is later respected
and further honoured
in inner councils

once he is chosen
above all other chiefs
to lead the forces
of the blackfoot confederacy
against piapot and 700 assiniboine
and cree—
300 to 500 of the enemy die
and bear child
leaves the battlefield
with 19 scalps
dangling from his belt—
this
the last battle among indians
of the northwest
and the end of bear child's
indian life

2

our guides
except for louis leveille
had all been hopeless—
a few of us rode
down to fort benton in 1874
we had heard of potts
that he was the finest guide
one could hope for
he joined us
the first day we arrived

the day we rode home
he rode far ahead of colonel french
and the rest of us—
when we caught up to him
in the evening
he'd already finished skinning
a young buffalo
there was a crystal spring nearby
and he'd already
started a campfire

there was something uncanny
about the way
he led us unfailingly
to different waterholes fed by springs—
one evening
by the fireplace at fort walsh
while we smoked and drank
colonel steele commented:
—*potts has a kind of sixth sense*
always knows where he is
in a blizzard or even
complete darkness

the winter of 1875
potts led four of us
from fort brisbois to helena montana
200 miles away—
we were picking up money ottawa had sent
for the force
on our first day
we arrived in fort macleod
and the wind was from the northeast—
it was a cold
and truly miserable day
and it continued to drift
out on the open prairie
all of the next day
on the third day the drifting
turning into a wailing storm
but potts wouldn't stop
finally
he led us down a bank of the milk river
it was evening
and the storm had worsened
and we couldn't see a thing
so we set up camp—

a small buffalo herd pressed in upon us
to seek shelter
by the river bank
we spent two days and nights
at that place
and it grew colder and colder
till some of the men began to panic
and were certain
we would freeze to death—
then potts decided
he would guide us to a shack
at rocky springs 30 miles away
while we rode south the storm
died down

but by the late afternoon the wind
rose again
and our tired horses stumbled along
our progress seeming
something mechanical
we followed potts
with our blind confidence
till it was twilight—
potts seemed a ghost from a dream
as he rode
in the storm ahead of us—suddenly
he reined his horse
to a halt
and slowly dismounted
riding up
we suddenly found ourselves
beside the shack
we had reached rocky springs
as potts groped for the doorhandle
we suddenly realized
he was nearly
completely snowblind

3

then there was the day
grayburn took his turn on herd duty
watching over our horses
three miles from fort walsh—
upon returning home late
in the afternoon
he realized he'd left
a lariat and axe behind
and returned
to retrieve the articles

that evening
when the young policeman didn't return
we sent out a search party—
when it grew too dark
the men finally returned
having found nothing

the following morning
i joined another search party
led by potts
a light snow had fallen
during the night
and the tracks had disappeared—
we circled the area
where we thought our horses
had been grazing
and coming to our tracks again
potts noticed
a bright patch of blood
within a hoof print—
he then rode south towards a tree
when we got there
we found a hat
hanging on a branch

beyond the tree
and down in the coulee
we found grayburn's body
then one of the men found the horse
tied to a branch
of a chokecherry tree
the horse had been shot
through the head—
potts silently circled the coulee
for a while
as we all waited
he then returned
having reconstructed all
that had happened—
he quietly mumbled:

they two injun
ride while with grayburn
slow down
when he ahead
shoot him in back
i questioned him:
how do you know this potts?
he replied:
three trail
two bare hoof mark
injun pony
grayburn trail deeper
his horse
have horse shoe

star child the murderer
was arrested
some time later—
a jury consisting of ranchers
found him *not guilty*
however
a few years later he received
five years
for horse stealing

4

me teach schofield be guide
teach him injun way

tole him:
wear buckskin
feel better
after day in saddle

teach him kindle campfire
injun way
use two three
small twig
put plenty buffalo chip round—
he laugh at me
first time i do this
i tole him:
damnfool whiteman
build big fire
stand long way off—
injun build small fire
squat down close

one evening we ride
jack rabbit jump up
over hill—
i take gun one hand
shoot him dead
one shot
funny schofield surprised—say:
jerry
where you learn to shoot that way?
i tole him:
you hungry
you shoot good

that night campfire burn low
we talk
drink bottle whiskey—
i put small piece buffalo fat
in coals
injun style
small fire wake up
i tole schofield
when fire die down:
this country
get too damn soft
for me

ELI LYCENKO

even in his grey eighties
when eli tied one on in the west central
he was a cougar tangled in barbed wire

he raged on to the day he died
and was obeyed and feared by all his children
even his slightest whim was a hailstorm
battering the hearts of those around him

they say when he fixed fence in the south pasture
every three years
he was always tempted by the old widow in the coulee
across pana's hill—
they claim she always arrived at the coulee's edge
her dress naughtily riding above buxom thighs
and she would say to eli
who would suddenly notice her in the distance:
you like eli? you want?
and old eli sweating under the high august sun
would suddenly twist his cap sideways
and tug his grizzled beard in brief bewilderment
the usual butt falling from his twisted mouth—
and once again the widow would beckon eli:
you like eli? you want?
and then rage would blur all things in eli's eyes
while he flung pliers to the ground
always exclaiming to himself: *woont i be a goddamn!*
before reaching for the nearest stone to heave
her way (and miss as usual) only to flush out another
pheasant in the nearby rosebushes

ERNIE HUDSON

ernie hudson
world war one veteran who returned to wood mountain
and later carried mail south to the old post
was once caught in a blizzard in the thirties
was pinned under his overturned sleigh and survived
while the team waited—someone arriving in the morning

his frozen right leg was amputated
and something died within him

in my boyhood
he was proorok (old biblical prophet) gathering beer bottles
on crutches always walking the south road
while i stuck to the north and west roads—
hunting for bottles early one morning following a dance
i saw a sudden wind gather the dust of main street
into a cloud (ernie disappearing to mysteriously reappear
by bloiun's store
ernie a ghost walking on air)

ernie was 80
when he crumpled with his first stroke
and i sold the regina *leader-post* for him
friday mail nights in hoy's place
till he returned from the hospital
something inside him changing once again—
ernie mellowed and began to attend church
with his frail wife
then the postmaster in wood mountain

a year later he was baptized
and i was grateful to be his fourteen year old godfather

LEE SOPARLO
for all the soparlos

ง

1 lee

in my boyhood i remember him as the skilful crossmaker
the cross always made from a four by four painted blue
the shade of billy brown's rodeo shirt
and the black plywood text carefully cut with a fretsaw

in the romanian church steeped in holy incense
the cross was always there among the mourners
and reverend erina praying
near the table heavy with loaves of sweet braided bread
the village children and the hungry froshhog boys and i waited for

in recent years he records names and dates of people's departures
births marriages and deaths in the region—
in another old scribbler
he records the years when the homesteaders arrived

now except for the trails end and a store
his house family and post office are the only sign of life
on main street—
monday to friday 7 a.m. he drives his school bus to the reserve
to pick up billy goodtrack's sons
and then continues south taking the shortcut along
the wood mountain–fort walsh trail to the old post

on dream's edge he fights the sleep in his aging eyes
while old settlers' ghosts loom up from the shadows
in the poplar forest along sitting bull hill

2 his father

his father was a blacksmith
and was later known as the depression dentist
who used angle iron to shape fearful pliers for extracting
molars and other teeth

he pulled his children's teeth during the thirties

they say men rode his way ten miles in a blizzard
to drink a quart of his homebrew
before lying down on his floor
where old soparlo would delicately press a knee on a man's chest
the left hand firming gripping the jaw
the right deftly yanking out still another molar—
sometimes only after wrestling the man on the floor
for an hour
both working up a good sweat
while soparlo shouted: *jeezuz—you sure you want it out?*
"yes—yesss
but maybe just another cup of homebrew first"

3 his brother

three elevators on the edge of wood mountain village
and john soparlo's the last one
bisecting the north-south road allowance

and i remember mother's biblical story about three men
one on the edge and how he ascended darkness and was saved

i remember the three hungry froshhog boys
and how we picked beer bottles around the elevator
and how the rare green beer bottle was something
to treasure

and we often watched john ride the manlift in the elevator
marvelled at the mysterious way
he disappeared high into the darkness to later return
from a place we could never go (or see)
and sometimes we waited and saw him return
his clothes face and eyes covered with a delicate fine dust
unlike anything we knew
except for that on the wings of a moth
i once shook from a green pilsner bottle

RORY NICHOLSON

the great wind dying down that day
the crickets' song shrill
in your ears
and the truck's skidmarks a bruise on the edge
of the coulee as you
turned for home to get help
for your father fighting the pain in his chest
as the last bit of sun
wedged between earth and sky at sundown
pierces the eye—
these became a testament bearing you from
boyhood to man
the meaning of father resting square and heavy
on your young shoulders
tears streaming back
while the gathering wind hugged the cab
as your father faded in uncle john's arms
beyond the grey plume of dust
you glimpsed in the mirror

DUNC AND BABE MCPHERSON

we notice so little in our lives
i think
looking again at their photograph taken
that sunday afternoon last fall
they standing arm in arm before the flower box
nailed beneath the window
and they cast a single shadow across the wall where
the washtub hangs next to the hammer on a nail—
i now notice in the foreground
the large flat stones half the length of a man
and <u>try to imagine</u> the energy it took to place them there
(something in the picture turns the mind to the visit
and how we entered their house—dunc saying:
the smell of your pipe makes me lonely for the old days
when i smoked my pipes

sitting down in his easy chair
dunc gazed a moment at the floating particles moving
through a light shaft angling down to the floor—
then he recalled their first experiences
when he and philip well were blacksmiths east of the old post:
i was shaping shoes when i heard horses whinnying
i looked up and there was babe
holding the reins of her father's team
that moment i said to myself "this lil lady's my wife"
and i tell you the honest God's truth andy
i've never looked at another woman since—yes
it was pure and simple as that
babe chuckled while she poured coffee: *yes and*
i was so afraid of him then
all i could say was "my daddy wants you to shoe these horses
please"

dunc talked about tire crimping the old forgotten craft
and the way he heated iron tires red hot
to crimp them with the two huge vices
how in busy times babe often helped him
throw the hot metal rings back on wooden wheels
suddenly immersed in a water trough to keep the wood from burning
dunc remembered how once a year
news arrived about a certain horserancher coming to have
his team shod:
they would jump half their height straight in the air—
the night before he arrived
i smoked myself hoarse andy and i even loaded a pipe
to calm myself in the middle of the night
when i woke up shaking from nightmares about them
dunc compares shoeing horses to tuning a banjo
and says one can tell by the sound of the nail
if one is doing it wrong and hurting the horse)

returning to their photograph
i notice how the garden has been extended
beyond the old fashioned well
note how they extended their boundaries
to include the abandoned house turned into a guest house
and i praise their full happy life here
where they found everything they ever needed
here in wood mountain where the stars are still distinct

to arrive at the final questions
leaving home for the other home some called more real—
and what takes greater courage?
a man depriving death of a dance to a grave in the spring
by his own hand?
or the rancher down in the badlands
ordering final things and transferring land titles
and building a new house to leave
the wife and children?
while something nudges up through the upper jaw
cattle fighting roosters and wild horses
that will one day invade the brain
something altering the taste of beer with boyhood buddies
while joking of the other man who knew days were numbered
and composed a verse over beer
to laugh and blow foam into the face of death:
"they say there's eternity
they say there's a heaven
and they say there's a hell
but you never can tell
and if you should go by in that old black hack
i'll kiss your ass if you ever come back"
the other man who drank and joked the whole winter
and was found on a sunny spring morning
swinging from a baling wire in the stockyards
his feet pointing northeast
moving in rhythm to a meadow lark's song

ODE TO THE OLDEST BROTHER

they have always called it *going home*
going home for christmas or easter
or even a funeral—
and although your way is not mine
we arrive here by mere chance
in this half deserted village
both home or what we call home
to visit our mother

merely one week later
i have had enough of childhood ghosts
and stories
of your misspent years and fights
with father and all those things
on the farm
and enough of your vodkalogged ghosts—
we have nothing to talk about
any more
and the silence
as you thumb through another copy of *jughead*
only confirms that we are strangers
to one another—
and isn't it a bit sad tonight
our mother 74 going over to a neighbour to bring you
a toronto security guard
home—mother
carrying your case of *bohemian lager* beer through the playground
where no children play
you 49
slowly staggering behind—

and isn't it a bitch being too drunk
unable to walk to the graveyard again tonight
and cry over the grave of the romanian sweetheart
you left to go to the war
your sweetheart who married
and to whom in '45 you returned
to fuck in the coulee by the ball diamond
on a friday mailnight
while her husband drank beer
in the pub

brother—i don't want to see
another bottle of *bohemian lager* beer
for the rest of my life
and am leaving home once again now—
only a funeral will bring me
back this way

LOUIS LEVEILLE

what they call civilization
pouf! look at me louis leveille
i have found everything right here
even love

he is 106 now
in 1973
his memory perfectly clear
like a honed diamond
while he is interviewed
in a movie

he speaks of wood mountain
and recalls minor battles with indians
as though they occurred yesterday

he rolls up his sleeves to show scars
where his arms
were grazed by blackfoot arrows

northern indians claim
he made birch bark canoes so light
they could float on a morning mist

LEAVING HOME

leaving home
i am always leaving home
leaving now the lot i thought was mine

leaving wood mountain
where wamblee* and his mate return
once a year from the badlands
to circle high over the old post—wamblee's shadow
huge enough to span indian graves

leaving now
the lone hunter from the reserve
his .303 often left on the village edge
he often forgetting where he left it
simply walking down this path
through this lot
passing this telegraph office here
no messages arrive
till wind rises—lone hunter
of whom they say:
he is dangerous
he is inhabited by two people
and i am one of them
afraid
and ashamed
leaving the lot and all that was
always his

leaving home having arrived
at the last of all follies
believing something here was mine
believing i could return
and build a home
within the dying

leaving home and shugmanitou
the cry of the hounds
drawing nearer

*wamblee: eagle in dakota

NIGHTBUS TO VANCOUVER

the busdriver nods into sleep
as we make another perfect curve
on our descent
into kicking horse canyon—
i am unafraid as i watch the mirror
and the driver fighting sleep
i am resigned
and no longer distinguish the real
from the unreal

since medicine hat
a farmer in the backseat laughs
and mumbles an unintelligible dialogue
between himself and two brothers
who died back in the thirties—
sleep is difficult
for the hippie couple head of him
as they nervously waken from dreams
of the tough eden highway

beside me sits an old man
too thin for adjectives
he too drifts into sleep
a cigarette smouldering in his hand
falling slowmotion
as the hand comes to rest on his leg
cloth begins to burn
(then swifter than barn swallows
the other hand extinguishes burning cloth—
he then lights another smoke
and coughs into sleep
as our bus bucks the wind down the deep canyon
to golden)

the next day in vancouver
i buy a paper and look for a place to live
finally find a room in the westend
(it's clean
big
and the landlord says
the walls are freshly papered
i take it for a mere $55 a month—
taking a second look around
i note further details:
recently painted ceiling and windowframes
a dozen or more burnt marks
where cigarettes have fallen
on the floor next to the bed)

too tired to unpack
i draw the curtains & lie down to sleep
a while—
as walls & darkness enfold me
i float thru a dream. . . .
the laughing face of the prairie madman
looms beyond flames rising on the edge of my bed

WESTERN PRAYER

time poet
to put aside what you came to
leaving all else
behind

time to unsaddle
this lame horse ridden
into ancestral dust
and cease living like an indian
of old

time to do things with the hands
working all seasons
with pride
and three weeks vacation
each year

time to tie this dream horse to a star
and walk
ordinary earth

ABOUT THE AUTHOR

Andrew Suknaski was born on a farm just outside the village of Wood Mountain in 1942. His mother came from Poland, his father from the Ukraine, which meant that his first contact with English was when he went to school. After leaving home at an early age, he turned his hand to an impressive range of occupations throughout the west (his official job description is "migrant worker"). He also filled in his education at universities here and there, and travelled as far afield as Europe and Australia.

For some years now he has been publishing poems in a wide variety of literary magazines, and in chap-books. These appearances brought him to the attention of Al Purdy, who included some of Suknaski's poetry in his anthology, *Storm Warning*, and offered to work with him to prepare a collection of his best work. *Wood Mountain Poems* is the result.

Of this collection Andrew Suknaski has written: "For me *Wood Mountain Poems* is a return to ancestral roots in my birthplace, after seventeen years of transience and aberration in numerous Canadian cities—and of trying to find the meaning of home." The poems also deal with "a vaguely divided guilt; guilt for what happened to the Indian (his land taken) imprisoned on his reserve; and guilt because to feel this guilt is a betrayal of what you ethnically are—the son of a homesteader and his wife who must be rightfully honoured in one's mythology". The book celebrates a third group, "the memorable characters who people my boyhood memories and whose Sioux, Roumanian, English, Ukrainian, or Serbian pride moved them to tell a well-remembered story".

This first major collection of Andrew Suknaski's poetry will also be well remembered.

ACKNOWLEDGEMENTS

Some of these poems appeared in *Antigonish, Another Poetry Magazine, Canada Goose, Capilano Review, Copperfield, Descant, Harbinger, New: Canadian & American Poetry, Northern Journey, Sailing the Road Clear, Salt,* and *Seven Persons Repository,* and in the following chapbooks: *Leaving Wood Mountain* (Sundog Press), *Philip Well* (New Caledonia Writing Series), *Wood Mountain Poems* (Anak Press), and *On First Looking Down From Lions Gate Bridge* (Black Mass Press).

With the assistance of helpful librarians, some of the poems began in the Edmonton City Library, the Edmonton Journal Microfilm Archives, the Glenbow Archives, and the Peter Whyte Library and Archives (in Banff, Alberta).

The author is grateful to the Canada Council for two short-term grants, and to Al Purdy and Dennis Lee for invaluable encouragement.

Finally, the author remains eternally grateful to Lee Soparlo, postmaster of Wood Mountain, who remembered most of the stories. Lee Soparlo is both Wood Mountain's and the author's memory.

LIST OF PHOTOGRAPHS

Cover Photograph: Sitting Bull. Courtesy of the Glenbow-Alberta Institute

Cover Photograph: Wood Mountain, by William Johnson

Cover Photograph: Andrew Suknaski, by Gerard Malanga

Page 1: Jerry Potts. Courtesy of the Glenbow-Alberta Institute

Page 3: Ox team breaking the prairie. Courtesy of the Glenbow-Alberta Institute

Page 6: Pioneer sod home in the Wood River district. Courtesy of the Saskatchewan Archives Board

Page 9: Homesteaders. Courtesy of the United Church of Canada Archives

Page 10: Sitting Bull. Courtesy of the Glenbow-Alberta Institute

Page 13: Ploughing with horses. Courtesy of the Glenbow-Alberta Institute

Page 123: Wood Mountain Roumanian Orthodox Cemetery, by William Johnson

Page 126: Wood Mountain Cafe and Confectionery, by William Johnson

Page 128: Trails End Hotel, by William Johnson